**infomediaplus**

Presents

# HOW TO START YOUR OWN BOUNCE HOUSE BUSINESS
# U.S.A.

## FROM PART TIME TO FULL TIME IN NO TIME

**infomediaplus**

For legal reasons we are obliged to state the following:

Disclaimer: To the fullest extent permitted by law, the sellers are providing this written material, its subsidiary elements and its contents on an 'as is' basis and make no (and expressly disclaim all) representations or warranties of any kind with respect to this material or its contents including, without limitation, advice and recommendations, warranties or merchantability and fitness for a particular purpose. The information is given for entertainment purposes only. In addition, we do not represent or warrant that the information accessible via this material is accurate, complete or current. To the fullest extent permitted by law, neither the sellers or any of its affiliates, partners, directors, employees or other representatives will be liable for damages arising out of or in connection with the use of this material. This is a comprehensive limitation of liability that applies to all damages of any kind, including (without limitation) compensatory, direct, indirect or consequential damages, loss of data, income or profit, loss of or damage to property and claims of third parties.

Copyright Graeme Renwall

All rights reserved. No reproduction, copying or transmission of this publication, CD's or DVD included in this system may be made without written permission. No paragraph of this publication may be reproduced, copied or transmitted without written permission, or in accordance with the Copyright Act 1956 (amended).

This course is sold for entertainment purposes only, and the author, publishers and/or distributors are not responsible for any actions taken as a result of reading this course.

**ISBN-13: 978-1477557808**

**ISBN-10: 1477557806**

**W**elcome and a very big 'Thank You' for purchasing this complete information system designed to save you a lot of time and money. I know you're going to be thrilled by the contents as I share with you my experiences and tips taken from over 10 years in the inflatable business.

Let me start by briefly taking you back to the start of how it all began.

# Introduction:

Originally the company started by chance; I was working as an Area Sales Manager for a major Bank. The hours were long and although the monetary rewards were good, the pressure and lack of free time was making me miserable. My wife was having our first baby, and wanted to give up her full time job which financially added to those pressures, (sound familiar). We decided, like a lot of people, to look for something different purely on a part time basis that could be run from home, to provide an additional income.

We looked at many different franchises, but found the majority wanted substantial investment, or involved the pressures I was trying to avoid. But we persevered and the strange thing is that when you're looking for something, something invariably turns up. A very good friend of ours (a home hairdresser) happened to cut the hair of another lady who lived quite near to us. Her name was Sandy and she had been successfully running a part-time bouncy castle business from home for ten years. Her goal was to educate her children privately. Unfortunately for us she and her husband had recently decided to sell off the stock of 'Sandy Castles' and use the funds to invest in a new venture. Although we had missed the boat in terms of buying her stock, they very kindly invited us over so we could "pick their brains" about the business. The information we gained that day was invaluable, but was the only research we ever did. This was a business for us, that sounded simple to provide, with minor outlay and that we could run from home part-time. Thus "Castles InThe Air" was formed.

We started by investing in four brand new bouncy castles in June 1998 which we stored in the garage. I had recently bought an old cheap Land Rover with the purpose of deliveries in mind, and after placing a small advert in the Yellow Pages phone Directory we sat back and waited for the phone to ring. The amazing thing about this business is the demand; we found ourselves inundated with calls throughout the summer. All of the castles went out Saturdays and Sundays plus some during the week. Within approximately ten weeks, the castles had paid for themselves. Not bad for a new business run with little experience.

What I found was that my customers were actually pleased to see me, something I hadn't been used to in corporate life. Most people were helpful, polite and desperate for that castle to entertain the kids. Without it the party could be a disaster. You would assume that nobody needs an inflatable throughout the winter but children's birthdays are all year round and many people hire halls for the occasion, thus making bouncy castles more than just a seasonal business.

Since June 1998 we have expanded and now own 20 inflatables, we service at least 750 customers per year, and supply for both children and adults. The beauty of the industry is that it allows you to choose your own level of both investment and reward. I know people locally who rent out one castle on a part time basis, and I know people who hire out over 40 units. The choice is yours.

I will touch on diversification later but bear in mind that the entertainment industry is vast so there is huge potential for expansion in this market. <u>Be advised however that the bigger the growth, the bigger the headaches and not necessarily the bigger the profit.</u>

Finally, if I had money for every time the man of the house had questioned me about the business angle, I would be a very rich man indeed. Fortunately for us the majority of people don't take it any further but the interest generated was one of the main reasons for writing this manual.

Unless you are very wealthy and this sounds like a good hobby, please do not run before you can walk. You should have goals and aspirations of course but everybody will have their own reasons for embarking on this venture and it's important to control this business rather than let it control you.

So in the future you will have three options:

1. To continue expansion, investment and establish a bigger market.
2. To sustain the current level and use the time available throughout the quieter months (e.g. winter) to diversify into other areas.
3. Can be a part time business only.

For now we will concentrate on the basics.

# Graeme Renwall.

PLEASE NOTE THAT IT IS STRONGLY RECOMMENDED THAT YOU CONTACT THE FIRE MARSHAL'S OFFICE IN YOUR STATE OR THE RELATIVE GOVERNING BODY OF YOUR COUNTRY TO CONFIRM ALL THE RULES AND REGULATIONS PERTAINING TO YOUR AREA BEFORE STARTING YOUR NEW BUSINESS VENTURE.

SECONDLY I AM NEITHER AN ACCOUNTANT NOR AN ATTORNEY/LAWYER SO PLEASE MAKE SURE THAT YOU SEEK THE APPROPRIATE FINANCIAL AND LEGAL ADVICE ON ALL THE RELATED ASPECTS OF THIS BUSINESS, PARTICULARLY AS DIFFERENT COUNTRIES OR STATES WILL HAVE DIFFERENT LAWS AFFECTING IMPLEMENTATION.

Thank you.

# KEYS TO SUCCESS:

Get some paper or use a computer with the following headers to start jotting down your own ideas. I have put some of mine below to help you begin.

**KEYS TO SUCCESS**:

- Excellence in achieving the promise, completely confidential, reliable and trustworthy.
- Offering a better service than other similar businesses.

COMPANY SUMMARY:

- We are a company that provides high-quality service to its customers in a local area.
- As it grows, the opportunity to employ people will be available, allowing the company to expand or diversify.

OBJECTIVES:

(a) Business expansion 20% each year.
(b) 95% Customer satisfaction.
(c) 75% Repeat custom.
(d) 15% Referral (word of mouth).

SERVICES:

We simply offer a variety of inflatables for hire to all ages, in a localised area. This includes schools, societies and charities, although our company mainly deals in residential demand.

MARKET ANALYSIS SUMMARY:

Our target market consists mainly of local residents who require inflatables for their children's parties etc.

MARKET SEGMENTATION:

Currently the cost of hiring an inflatable ranges from **X** to **X** per day. Therefore our market is virtually anyone locally, regardless of income.

DELIVERY & COLLECTION:

Repeat custom is very important in this type of business, so all of the aspects that were considered when taking the bookings should be considered when delivering and collecting the inflatable. Making a mess of delivery or collection times loses you business and harms your reputation.

STRATEGY AND IMPLEMENTATION SUMMARY:

We will continue to focus on our localised area. By using our simple techniques in both advertising and communication skills we intend to concentrate on our existing customer base for repeat business and referrals for future business. By continuing slowly to add different products, we will always be able to offer versatility and choice which when combined with our 'service philosophy' gives us the edge against our competitors.

COMPETITIVE EDGE:

There are simple ways which can give your company a competitive edge; these include :

* Reliability
* No charge if not set-up due to bad weather
* Clean and well maintained inflatables
* Service with a smile
* On call help if required

SALES STRATEGY:

Sales in our business means client service. We must be aware of the competition and the importance of not only selling the job but also fulfilling our promises.

FINANCIAL PLAN:

a) We want to finance growth mainly through cash flow. We recognise this means we may grow more slowly than we would like.

The most important factor in our case is payment on delivery and therefore we are never in a weak cash flow position.

WEB PLAN SUMMARY:

The website is used for three main reasons:

- To gain new customers from the internet by ranking highly in my area.
- To allow both old and new customers to view our products, prices and sizes, terms and conditions, safety procedures, deposit instructions, items for sale etc. etc.
- It allows us to update our products and services using a fast and cost effective method.

O.K.  That should get the juices flowing....................................

# MARKETING

The first section I want to discuss in detail is **Marketing**, particularly on a tight budget. Let's assume you have already ordered your first one or two bouncy castles and they are due to arrive shortly. From now on, if you see the word **(Toolbox)** in brackets, please refer to the Toolbox section which contains website addresses and information that I personally use and that will help **you** save a lot of money and time.

In my opinion (and yes I am guilty of not following my own advice on occasion), treating each customer like gold dust is the key to the success of any business but **particularly this one.** Remember that this is *your* time and money invested now. It all starts with.......

THE PHONE CALL (Feedback over the years):

Virtually all of my bookings are taken over the phone, and therefore it is vital that you maintain the following:-

- Where possible, answering the phone (rather than diverting to answer phone) - caller may go elsewhere and does. There is nothing that frustrates me more than losing business to competitors simply because I missed a call. If you go out then divert the phone to a mobile. It will cost you a bit more but the return will be worth it.
- Good phone manner (polite, helpful and upbeat). This doesn't mean sound like a clown but it does mean sound positive and keen. That's common sense I hear you say but believe me, this attitude costs you nothing but will win you customers from your 'less than keen' competition.
- Be confident, in other words know your stuff. This will come with experience but practice before going live, **(Toolbox).**
- Be as helpful as possible.
- Be flexible (this may include price, and other aspects such as time of delivery etc). You are just starting so you want to try and be one of if not the most competitive. In this economic climate, people are very price sensitive but don't go too low as this could suggest a substandard product/service.
- Be thorough when taking information. I have designed an **Order Form** for just this purpose located at the back of this manual.

Each party or event is a chance for you to develop more business through word of mouth. So arrive on time or earlier if possible for delivery. This gives you more time to sell yourself and the company to the customer, will put you under less pressure so you come across more relaxed and if something does go wrong, you will have the time to hopefully put it right. Basically have a laugh with them where possible and try to leave the inflatable for longer than previously agreed or even overnight if viable. This will leave a good impression of value for money and the customer will come back again and again.

GENERAL MARKETING:

All of the following suggestions have been tried and tested by myself with varying degrees of success. I have removed the ones that didn't work by the way. Choose whatever suits your situation based on time and finances.

Tell everyone what you do, news travels fast. Have friends over to see your castle, offer a small discount to them and their family if you wish. If possible hand out business cards **(Toolbox)** to them.

Place an advert in the Yellow Pages. New businesses usually get a good discount and the rep. can advise you on the best places to position the ad. I also advertise in smaller local magazines/newspapers that are designed for parents looking for ideas to entertain children.

Contact local business in a similar field as you i.e. entertainers and face painters, then offer to pass on their number to your customers; ask them to do the same for you. These days you can just email them on the web.

Offer a free hire to local primary schools, playgroups, day care centres, large businesses or hospitals on the condition that they hand out leaflets promoting your company.

Put a sign (magnetic, **(Toolbox)** sticky or just typed) in/on your van/car windows, promoting what you do.

Take something free for the customer when you arrive. For example a fridge magnet with 'Happy Birthday' on it plus all your contact details. **(Toolbox)** or a birthday card. This will help you get further bookings and is a nice touch.

Take an interest on the telephone when customers ring, taking the time out to ask about their party, not just simply giving a price. It is nice to speak to someone pleasant when you are planning your child's party, and above all, emphasise that you are reliable, professional, and that your castles are safe.

Deliver fliers, business cards or postcards **(Toolbox)** in the streets around your area. Make sure that this is legal in your state first. Hard work I know but it does work and keeps you fit!!

Keep your diary safe and 6-8 weeks before their party is due next year, send them a flier or a letter reminding them of your phone number with perhaps a special offer or better still an email, (see order form for email capture). Naturally if you are a whizz on the computer you can access and update all your records quickly and accurately.

Use Toolbox for one of the most cost effective forms of advertising on the planet.

THE WEB:

I'm afraid, yes you do need a website and a printer. Now hopefully, like I did originally, you know someone who will do it for you for free or swap you for the hire of a castle. This is great but unless it's a very good friend or a member of the family, you will find that the following will occur. Whenever it needs updating or altering not only will you have to ask for another favour but it will never be done as quickly as **you** want. Secondly if you fall out with the person, it isn't that easy to regain control. I speak from experience so think wisely before you choose this option. Thirdly and in my opinion most importantly, having a website is great for showing customers what you have to offer and the prices but absolutely useless for creating new business. These days you need to be on the front page of Google when someone searches for a bouncy castle in your area.

The second option is to look on the net for a designer. Could be expensive but a lot of people use www.elance.com for a cheaper alternative.

This manual was not created to show you how to develop websites or rank highly for search engines but I will tell you what I have done in the last few months.

First of all I am not a computer geek. Like most people I traditionally used it for emails, facebook, youtube and general information. But I have now bitten the bullet. Using a specific program **(Toolbox)** which is not free but it is amazing, I can now design my own. I can update it whenever I want to in seconds. I can change the look of it and use it as a database for all my clients should I want to send out a special offer, the list is endless and once you buy it that's it, it's yours for life. There is a fantastic tutorial which even I could follow and although daunting at the beginning, my friends and family are now astounded. Not bad for a 44 year old. I have included a cheaper alternative in (**Toolbox)** which may also be of interest to you so do not panic. Another tip I would strongly recommend once your website is up and running is writing articles to ezines (magazines on the net) e.g. www.ezine.com, which dramatically improves your ranking and costs nothing.  If you don't like writing articles or feel that you can't then join www.needanarticle.com, these days anything can be done for you. I use www.hostgator.com as my host who I personally find extremely helpful, reliable and cost effective.

The last chapter on this subject is Google Adwords. You can actually pay for your website to be advertised when somebody types in key words. Go to www.adwords.google.com for further information.

(Incidentally if you don't have satellite navigation (like me), use the maps section above the Google toolbar, click directions, type in where you are going and it gives you all of them from A to B for FREE. Print it off for the delivery but always take a local map with you for backup).

"Be creative and try anything" to promote your business is my motto.

# NUTS AND BOLTS

The second section I have entitled **Nuts and Bolts** as it aims to cover everything else I have learned or researched to make your life easier.

CHOOSING A NAME:

This is the fun part. It's pretty easy thinking of a catchy name but the trouble is other people may have thought of it already. Make sure that it hasn't been taken first and protected by federal, state or country trademark rights **(Toolbox).** You don't want to be sued in your first week! Once you have found a name that has not been registered go to www.godaddy.com or similar registration site and confirm that the domain name is available so you can use it for your website.

**Tip: A name starting with A or B will get you nearer the top in a phone directory & a catchy phone number (i.e. 555-BOUNCE) will help people remember you.**

CHOOSING A DELIVERY VEHICLE:

I currently own a Ford Transit van that I bought second-hand. With the volume of castles I now hire out, I need the long wheel base model for the extra space it gives. As mentioned earlier, the bigger inflatables are particularly heavy but in the early days I used an old Land Rover successfully to deliver 4 units on a part-time basis. Any truck or trailer will do providing it is legally allowed to carry the weight.

As I expanded the business, a very good friend allowed me to borrow his Toyota van which again did the job. Later before buying my own transport, I hired a bigger van for weekends only which worked out to be excellent value.

To summarise, I didn't just rush in and by a fleet of transport vehicles! Remember always that transport represents a large part of overall costs in this business and consequently you should start with the smallest and cheapest you can find, until your business can support something better.

**Tip: If buying a van, having it boarded out inside (e.g. plywood) makes life so much easier and protects the interior.**

STORAGE:

I have used a normal sized garage at home since the beginning for convenience and to save on costs. You will however need space to inflate your castles for repairs, drying or general inspection. I have personally used my garden for this purpose but again it depends on how many castles you have. You may decide you need something bigger like a barn or a warehouse - shop around, ask your friends if they know anyone who is looking to rent out storage space. You may be pleasantly surprised.

**Tip: Always, always, always** store your castles on top of wooden pallets. This allows the air to circulate underneath them. It also allows any excess water to fall away until such time as you are able to thoroughly dry the unit. Usually pallets are easy to obtain either cheaply or if you look around free of charge. Check DIY stores or Builders Merchants who often have pallets they can spare or want to get rid of. I have never paid for a wooden pallet.

SPACE REQUIRED:

**Outdoors**

Again experience in the field saves time, money and avoids disappointment. Once you get used to the size of each castle you own, and have erected them a few times, you will be able to gauge on the phone whether the customer has sufficient room for that particular unit. Occasionally I have popped around to the house to check for myself if local. Good customer service again.

It's important to know both the length and width of each castle but more importantly the height. Sometimes customers have trees or other objects in the garden which may cause difficulties. Be aware that most inflatables have a hose or tube at the back which connects to the blower or fan. Therefore the extra length required including the safety mat positioned at the front of the castle, must be discussed prior to the booking of the appointment. At least 6 feet extra (1.83m) to the length of the inflatable is a sensible requirement and to be safe, an extra 2 feet (0.61m) in width to that of the unit also makes sense.

**Tip: Where possible, carrying a smaller sized castle on board for those unexpected problems can save the day!**

**Tip: The blower when attached to the tube at the back of the castle can be set at an angle without compromising the pressure. This could gain you valuable inches if required in a confined space.**

**Indoors**

Mainly halls or clubs where the above applies but pay particular attention to height. Some halls have very low ceilings or beams.

OVERNIGHT DROPS:


Depending on the size of your business and the type of events you focus on, it may be sometimes lucrative or helpful to leave an inflatable overnight. For example, if it is pouring with rain and the castle is not required the following day, leaving it with the customer could make sense. Also, you may get bookings to hire a castle for two days plus or be involved in the adult market where the parties usually go on all night.


Whatever the reason, leaving a unit overnight may occur in which case you need to be aware of vermin. Fortunately for me (and I leave a lot of castles overnight) there have only ever been two attacks, both on the same castle. I was able to repair the castle myself on both occasions but the vermin did a lot of damage. Perhaps this particular unit had a scent that attracted them, which cannot be eradicated. In any event, I have found the attacks to be extremely rare. A solution would be to ask the customer to cover the castle at night with a large groundsheet or tarpaulin to protect it. Most people are generally very helpful and do not want to be held liable for any damage caused.

**Tip: Ask the customer to inflate the unit the following day to help dry it off for collection - this will obviously depend on the weather! Explain that it will be too heavy to carry if the excess water is not removed.**

All these requests depend on the relationship you build with the customer, but 90% of them will always help if they can.

THE WEATHER:

I must confess that since being involved in the inflatable hire business, I have been addicted to checking the weather via the internet. Rain can be your worst enemy, leading to cancellations and therefore loss of sales. My policy on bad weather - very simply, we do not charge the customer if we don't set the castle up. Occasionally I have driven to a house for an appointment and been told they would prefer to cancel the booking. But generally the customer phones in the morning to discuss the various options available and probably saves you a journey. Either way we wouldn't charge. On the reverse side of this situation, if the customer gambles and takes the castle, we charge on delivery and erection even if the weather makes it impossible to use later on that day for example.

**THE WEATHER (Cont.)**

**PLEASE NOTE THAT YOU MUST NEVER SET UP A CASTLE IF YOU FEEL THAT THE WEATHER, PARTICULARLY THE WIND MIGHT MAKE THE INFLATABLE DANGEROUS TO USE.**

My advice would be to buy an inflatable with a detachable rain/shade cover. This allows the unit to be used in light rain, but never when heavy or persistent. Obviously if there are strong winds, thunder or lightning then the power should be switched off immediately and the castle not used.

A shower cover can also help protect against sunshine. Where possible, try to erect the castle in the shade as strong sunshine can make the plastic very hot for bouncing - wearing socks helps, of course, and is advisable. If the safety mat gets too hot, ask the customer to flip it over rather then spray water on it. The mats are made of foam and therefore absorb water making it difficult for them to be dried off.

Other companies do not necessarily follow our policy. Some charge a deposit up front or insist on a cancellation fee. The fairest way is to hold a deposit but allow the customer to use that deposit towards the cost next time they hire an inflatable. . Again choose the policy that suits your business, but bear in mind that a satisfied customer will probably come back next year!

## MOULD:

If you have ever owned a tent, you are probably aware that to leave it stored away wet for a long period of time causes mould. Bouncy castles unfortunately suffer the same fate.

Mould can be devastating - I learned the hard way and have spent many days cleaning various castles to combat this menace. It's hard work and not recommended. Make sure you inflate to dry off as quickly as possible. This may take a day or two depending on the time of year. Before putting a castle away, make certain that it is bone dry by feeling inside either via the tube or through the deflation zips. You may think the castle is dry on the surface, but inside is where it counts. Once positive, store the castle on top of a pallet, allowing air to circulate underneath.

As per our Terms and Conditions (see back of manual), you will see although we endeavour to deliver our inflatables in a dry condition, this is not always possible (due to the weather from the previous day for example). Customers should allow the castle to dry before using it, as slippery beds can cause accidents. We always carry dry towels to remove excess water quickly from the bouncing area immediately after erection.

SUPERVISION AND COLLECTIONS:

*Supervision:-* One area that I have dabbled in is the supervision market e.g. supplying schools, fetes, boot sales, weddings etc. and actually staying to supervise whilst charging each child to bounce. I know people that do this regularly and can take a lot of money if the weather is kind and the venue has a strong turn out. There are some inflatables that an insurance company will only cover if supervised, Bouncy Boxing and Giant Slides to name a couple. Personally I found it extremely hard work and very boring. Continually monitoring other people's children of all ages is not easy; I prefer to leave it to the parents who are giving a private party, but again the choice is yours! You can certainly offer supervision as a selling point but remember that your time is valuable and you should therefore charge accordingly.

**Tip: If you decide to supervise, always carry a whistle.**

*Collections*:- There is always the temptation to allow a complete stranger/customer to collect an inflatable, set it up themselves, and bring it back to you. I have done this a few times in the past but would advise against it. Firstly my public liability insurance no longer allows it. I am personally responsible for ensuring that each castle set up has been checked and is safe for use, (this keeps the cost of the premium lower too). Secondly you cannot check the state of an inflatable if returned already rolled up and unfortunately one was returned to me damaged. It wasn't a serious tear but it made me decide to never do it again.

STAFF:

Employing people to help you will depend on how big your business grows. My advice is to speak to an accountant before starting, to confirm the tax implications. Once you feel confident about setting up your inflatables on your own, you will need to train someone new if you require help with deliveries. You must be satisfied that the individual is fully competent before allowing them to represent your company and document all the training given. This could take many weeks of supervision but it's well worth the effort.

The method of staff payment differs from company to company. Some pay by the day a fixed fee, for example. Personally I prefer paying a set amount for each delivery and a set amount for each collection; then, if an inflatable is not delivered or not collected due to bad weather then nobody gets paid. My experience confirms that you get what you pay for. I would rather reward someone well who was reliable, intelligent and trustworthy, than pay less to someone who wasn't. Remember they are representing your company and future business could well depend on their actions.

Most of the people I have worked with have been friends or friends of friends. They don't necessarily need the money but enjoy the change of scene and

STAFF (CONT.)

the simplicity compared to their own varied careers. Some have been excellent but cannot afford the time on a regular basis, others have tried only once! Occasionally you meet people who are the perfect choice for the job, but it still takes time to train them. Make sure you treat them fairly, pay them well and support them as much as possible. As in all businesses the difficulty is finding the right people. Always be "on the look out" for prospective employees as in my experience, you can never have too many to call upon for the future.

WHAT TO BUY WHEN STARTING:

I started by buying 4 castles. They were "Mini Bounce" (8x10 feet or 2.44m x 3.05m), "Ball Bounce" (10x10 feet or 3.05m x 3.05m), "Dino" (12x12 feet or 3.66m x 3.66m) and "Basket Bounce (14x14 feet or 4.27m x 4.27m). These different sized castles meant that I had something that appealed to most age groups in the child market with general themes, i.e. clowns, balloons, friendly dinosaurs and basketball plus they all had shower covers.

**BUT THAT WAS THEN. TIMES HAVE CHANGED.**

I would now recommend what I call a slide bouncer. An inflatable with a slide attached for the younger age groups e.g. maximum age 10. My advice would be to buy two of these to begin with, one with a boy theme and one with a girl theme. Some manufacturers have special licences, **(make sure that they have before you buy)**, that allow them to paint specific images like Disney for example or Batman/Spiderman. These themes will probably <u>always</u> last and therefore <u>always</u> be in demand but so will Pirate themes for boys or pink and candy/puppies for girls. Ask the manufacturers which are their most popular themes? Why start with the younger age group? This will be your main demand but more importantly will cause you less wear and tear than the adult market i.e. less boisterous. Parents are far more concerned about their younger children generally when bouncing and are therefore more likely to monitor them carefully.

**Tip: The inflatable should be arched rather than flat as this allows the air to flow more freely in warmer weather, even with the cover on.**

WHAT TO BUY WHEN STARTING: (Cont.)

**The example below shows the type of inflatable I would recommend. Notice how there is no barrier to stepping on and off for the children. This makes it easier for supervision and easier for you to clean. Again make sure that this type or design of inflatable does not infringe any laws in your State. Another advantage in my opinion is that if there is a power cut or the blower malfunctions it is much easier to remove the children quickly unlike an enclosed bouncer.**

**5.18m (17 feet approx) Wide**

**4.27m (14 feet approx) Long**

**Why this type of combo?**

Trust me when I tell you that when potential customers see a bouncy castle with a slide, particularly with a popular boy or girl theme, the only thing they then consider is the price! If you are one of if not the cheapest in the area and you advertise this as an All Day Hire Special, the word

21

will spread fast. Always mention that **\*Conditions Apply\*** wherever you promote the offer as you will need to calculate the distance you are prepared to travel (fuel and time costs) and how many hours the customer is entitled to keep the inflatable for at this amazing price. Secondly the difference in cost of buying an inflatable combination like the one above as opposed to just a "bouncer" is negligible these days. Make sure that when buying a unit of this type that the "slide cover" is included in the price. This is usually detachable and will not only help to protect the slide but will give it a smoother surface. The one above has a **manufacturers** maximum age limit of **10** and a recommendation of no more than **8** kids at any one time. This may vary of course depending on where you purchase it but the theme itself suggests the younger age group.

This is exactly what you want.

When starting YOU DO NOT WANT or NEED a huge unit that takes 3 men to lift, especially when wet.

The importance here is to create the demand. Once someone is on the phone they are obviously keen to buy from you. The vast majority of people are very reasonable about the taking of deposits or being charged a little extra for distances outside your area. Most of the time I deliver between 6 a.m. and 10 a.m. but this will depend on the actual time of the party of course so be flexible. Then I agree to pick the castle up towards the end of the day or an hour after the party finishes. The beauty of this is that it leaves most of the day FREE.

Inflatable purchases will of course depend on your budget, but by contacting different manufacturers **(Toolbox)** you should be able to obtain many brochures full of numerous inflatable ideas plus get a good deal in the current climate.

As previously mentioned, make sure you start off on a small scale to see if the business is right for you! Buy one with an attached/stitched on shower/shade cover which can stop the children trying to climb the walls. Avoid anything to do with adding balls/water, e.g. a ball pond or anything else that may seem good on paper but in reality is time consuming for you to keep clean or to collect. Remember that even when rolled up, these units can be very heavy, particularly if wet so a good quality sack barrow or trolley is essential.

You will find that prices vary between manufacturers but cheap is not necessarily good. Check how long they have been in business making bouncy castles; this of course doesn't prove anything except some continuity. Always try and get a recommendation before buying new for peace of mind. Naturally a warranty and a certificate are essential to protect you as a consumer. Check what is included in the price **(Toolbox)**. Most companies provide electric fan, repair kit plus stakes to keep the castles secure on grass in the package, but don't be afraid to ask for extras like groundsheets, extension leads, safety mats or spare straps for securing castles once rolled. If you don't ask you don't get! Finally, once making an order be sure to confirm when it will arrive. You will probably be offered the option of having your name and phone number printed on the castle, this is a MUST.

**Tip: Use the boxes that the fans or blowers are delivered in. This will protect them in transit.**

SECOND-HAND MARKET:

I do have second-hand units but they weren't purchased until I had had 2 years experience in the business. Like all used goods it helps to know what to look out for! Check the pressure by bouncing on the inflatable personally. Does it feel strong? Is the artwork fading? Does all the stitching seem intact? How old is the castle? Is the manufacturer or seller reputable? Does it come with a certificate? Does the asking price include a fan, stakes or any other extras? Why are they selling? Is the theme and size what you are looking for?

Remember that most second-hand inflatables will have the name of the current owners and their telephone number painted on the front. This could lose you potential business of course.

As you can see there are a lot of questions to ask yourself before buying in this market. To find units for sale use the internet mainly but if your budget allows, I would recommend starting with some new stock.

HEALTH AND SAFETY:

If buying a new bouncy castle, the manufacturer should provide you with a certificate confirming that the castle conforms to the required standard of manufacture and which is valid for at least one year. It is then your responsibility to renew that certificate but not necessarily through the same manufacturer. You may want to take it to someone locally for inspection but again shop around on price. **Check the public liability guidelines carefully to ascertain the insurance company's conditions on this matter** as they may allow you to check the castle personally but again keep records and evidence to support this. Be advised that this is a "Health and Safety" requirement and therefore must be implemented regularly. This also applies to all your electrical devices also which includes the blower and extension leads. These should be checked by you every time you use them for any wear and tear signs but legally you will need to have them checked by a qualified electrician at least annually. Ask around locally as to the costs and legal requirements of your state.

ACCOUNTS:

Again, I repeat I am not an Accountant and would advise anyone starting a new business to seek expert advice in this field. One tip which might sound obvious is to set up a new bank account for the business but again shop around for deals, **particularly with banks**. I find by keeping things separate from my personal account and recording all outgoings using receipts as evidence, the job for my Accountant is made that much easier. This also helps to keep costs down !

THE YOUNGER AGE GROUP MARKET:

The bulk of my business is unsurprisingly aimed at children. Generally it is the manufacturer who stipulates the age limits of the castle although this can vary. Some of my castles are restricted to age 13 and some age 14. My public liability insurance assumes age 14 to be the upper age limit and anything over this falls into the adult category! Remember however that the height of the walls is a key issue-nobody standing on the bed of a bouncy castle should be taller than the outside walls. Therefore depending on the size of the castles you own, a degree of common sense is required when hiring out a particular unit.

You will see later from our "Order Form" that the information we obtain should be sufficient when making a recommendation. For example, you would not hire out a small inflatable to a 14th birthday party nor a huge bouncy slide to toddlers. These are extremes but hopefully illustrate my point.

ADULT MARKET:

Yes, there is an adult market! Big kids at heart I hear you say but you wouldn't believe the volume of enquiries we get.

Fewer bouncy castle companies in my experience get involved in this area however. I dabble currently by renting out a bouncy castle and an inflatable "Gladiator" unit for the over 14's. I charge a lot more for these units mainly because to insure them costs significantly more than those used for children but also as mentioned previously the wear and tear potential is greater.

My disclaimer clearly states that no-one under the influence of alcohol or drugs should be allowed on the inflatable at any time. My belief is that a lot of the claims made against bouncy castle companies/insurance companies have emanated from adults probably under the influence. Because of this, be aware that restrictions by insurance companies have increased particularly in this market. Check conditions imposed by public liability insurers first before buying any unit!

That aside, the adult market is buoyant and lucrative. Try judging on the phone first, whether the individual takes safety seriously-do not be afraid to point out the serious implications of drinking alcohol while bouncing, of overcrowding and of not supervising properly. Yes adults must also be supervised. If you feel uneasy in any way about the potential customer's manner or the conversation in general, don't risk hiring out - there are plenty more fish in the sea.

**Tip: If you do decide to invest in this category then always try to leave the unit overnight. Adult parties generally finish later anyway so it makes good sense.**

THE COMPETITION:

Like all good businesses, you may find that there are a lot of people advertising in your area to hire out inflatables. Do not be alarmed. Over the last 10 years competition has certainly increased, but there seems to be enough demand to go around. The trick is to keep working your market. Do not get complacent.

Compared to bouncy castles there are few things that can entertain children in my opinion at such a cost-effective price. Therefore because word of mouth is one of the best forms of advertising, the demand for inflatables is also increasing rapidly.

When starting in any venture, your instinct may be to try and beat the competition - there is nothing wrong in improving your volume of sales but my advice is to make friends and contacts in this business. Help where and when you can, within reason, and you will find that when you need help or are in trouble they will do the same. If you are fully booked then pass the lead to someone you know locally, making sure you tell the customer to say by whom they were recommended.

Like this manual, the sharing of best practices will only help to make your business grow quicker.

PUBLIC LIABILITY INSURANCE: **(Toolbox)**

Please be advised that I am not an expert on public liability insurance and that the following is based on my experiences. Anyone wishing to pursue this type of cover will be well advised to seek professional broker advice. Like all insurances worldwide, costs, cover, rules and regulations change frequently and differ between companies so, if possible look around for the best deal for you personally.

You won't be surprised to learn that the cost of public liability insurance has risen since I started. I assume the reasons for this have been due to more people entering the business. Also with the current ease of suing for any accident, claims have unfortunately substantially increased. Again I reiterate you must seek your own professional guidance in this area but I can advise you to:

1) Take out public liability cover for your business.

2) Read the policy carefully and ensure you fully comply with all its conditions.

3) Remember that when using a bouncy castle, there is the risk of accidents to be considered. Your priorities as the owner, are to ensure you have done everything in your power to provide safe, quality goods that are checked on

PUBLIC LIABILITY (CONT.)

the day of delivery. In addition to ensure that the customer has understood the safety issues involved and has signed paperwork confirming this.

As you read on, I hope you will agree that the structure of my business and the paperwork we use go a long way to protecting our customers and ourselves. Safety is paramount and by delivering this message you will only increase your referral business. The **TUTORIAL YOUTUBE VIDEO (O1) (TOOLBOX)** contained in this system was designed with this in mind and although nothing is foolproof, I hope that by following my example you can at least minimise the risks. *Remember I have never had a claim!*

DIVERSIFICATION :

The advantage of this industry is the flexibility and the demand. Flexible because you can choose your area, your volume of sales and the time you wish to spend on the business. Demand because I have found inflatable hire expands with very little effort. Just through delivering castles to a few parties, the referral/word of mouth process has helped me rapidly increase my profits!

You won't be surprised to hear that the real surge of enquiries happens in the warmer months. Other alternatives to supplement your income may include balloons for those special occasions, marquees or even just tables and chairs for hire. Sno-cone, cotton candy and popcorn machines are also popular. The advantage of some of these add-ons is that since they can be used indoors, they are not affected by inclement weather. Most customers like to hire everything from one place and by offering the complete package you stand a good chance of winning the business.

I have met children entertainers/magicians who are booked solidly throughout the year. Discos for children are also in great demand as are face painters and you would not believe the prices they generally charge per hour!

The point is that as always the choice is yours and the choices endless. Creativity is the key and not being averse to trying something new. But that's for the future!!

In the **Toolbox** you will find some phone numbers of places to contact for equipment and supplies. Always ask for a catalogue if one is available.

# BUILDING A LOCAL BUSINESS:

In a perfect world for this business, the smaller the area of delivery the better - less fuel used, particularly these days, means more profit; less distance travelled means more time for you. Again, this is my preference but if you decide to focus on the bigger jobs or the corporate market then it could be worth your while to travel greater distances. Assuming you start off on a smaller scale, how do you build up a local empire? The section on marketing gives you numerous options and ideas on how to get your company established. If you are professional, competitive and reliable the word soon gets around.

Naturally this can take time, but in my opinion choosing the areas you wish to concentrate on and giving yourself a strict radius initially will help you in the long term. When starting, most people are eager to please anybody that rings up just to get the booking, regardless of where it is. Remember this affects your profit margin both initially using fuel but longer term considering wear and tear! Generally children will invite a number of friends from their school to a party, thus the locality of referral business will be similar. You may be faced with future business calls in that area which could cause difficulties in peak times, to meet delivery and collection deadlines. Unfortunately it can be embarrassing to turn down referral business when you have already delivered to that area recently!

Like everything else you must be prepared to be flexible; generally I will travel much further in the quieter months, or when someone hires more than one inflatable at a time - sometimes I may add on the cost of fuel to cover my overheads. The point is to try and be structured in your approach by politely turning down business if it falls outside the catchment area you desire, or better still pass it on to the competition as previously mentioned.

28

# HOW TO CLEAN YOUR BOUNCY CASTLE:

Remember always to have the hire agreement signed and check the unit over when you collect. Should the castle be particularly dirty (this shouldn't happen) you need to discuss a cleaning charge with the customer as per signed agreement. Castles need minimal cleaning so long as the operating instructions are followed. Use of a groundsheet and a quick wipe over of any muddy or grubby parts when you collect (keep a damp cloth, sponge and dry towel in your vehicle-**Toolbox**) should minimise the cleaning of the unit as a whole. When however you do want to thoroughly clean your unit you can follow the steps below.

1. Pick a sunny, dry day to inflate and clean your castle.

2. See **Toolbox** for recommended cleaning solutions.

3. If the roof is particularly dirty, having deflated the castle, take off your shoes and clean the flattened material using water.

4. Spray the inner surface and walls with the cleaning solution **(Toolbox)**, one section at a time, drying off the sections as you go so that you don't get runs.

5. Clean the outside area next as above.

6. Finally vacuum clean inside the castle (this removes grass and sand etc) and finish off cleaning the inside.

7. See **Toolbox** for final touches.

8. Allow to blow for a while until dry before deflating and packing away.

9. If the castle gets soaked on a rainy day, store away on a pallet so that the water drains down as much as possible and get the unit out for a clean over and thorough drying as soon as possible. Storing wet castles is not recommended due to mildew.

**Tip: If you think it might be a while before you are able to inflate the wet castle, unfold it in a dry area such as a garage to the best of**

**your ability. Even if it won't unfold completely, at least the air will get to most of it reducing the chance of mildew setting in.**

**Tip: Most castles have a large zip at the back to help the air escape quickly. I often take a peek through this hole while the blower is still running just to check that the inside is bone dry before deflating. <u>Obviously care needs to be taken that the unit is not left unattended at this point in case a small child was to crawl in unnoticed! This could be dangerous.</u>**

The next two sections should be read in conjunction with the THE TUTORIAL YOUTUBE VIDEO (02) - TOOLBOX.

HOW TO ERECT A BOUNCY CASTLE:

1. You need to site the castle on clean, clear grass preferably. Slightly uneven ground is all right but not a steep slope as this could be dangerous. If placing on concrete you will need to secure to something heavy.

2. Inspect the ground and remove any debris. Place down the ground sheet.

3. Move the castle into place; using a sack trolley is an easy way of doing this. Place the castle in the centre of the ground sheet and unfold - turning the tube at this point into the place where you want the blower to be inflated (the rear).

4. Once the castle is unfolded, attach the blower, by opening the tube up and stretching across the funnel. Use a rope or strap to secure the funnel tightly in place.

5. Unwind the extension cable and plug into blower. Check that extension lead is not worn or chaffed and that there are no exposed wires. Check the blower also ensuring that nothing is loose or could cause a potential hazard.

6. Plug extensions cable into circuit breaker and then into mains. Test the circuit breaker using the 'TEST' button and if working correctly, switch on the power.

7. Once inflated, anchor the loops on the castle with heavy mallet and stakes - it is always best to make an additional small loop with strong rope so that the castle isn't pinned down too tightly, just so that it can move slightly and not cause a rip.

8. Ensure the cables are trailed away safely and taped down if necessary.

9. If you are using a petrol blower, you will need to regulate the motor adequately and check the oil.

10. You can now begin your safety check-over of the unit prior to the customer signing the agreement.

HOW TO PACK AWAY YOUR BOUNCY CASTLE:

1. Make sure the bouncy castle is completely empty of all children and any debris.

2. Switch off the electrical supply and disconnect the blower. Unzip any other outlets available.

3. Allow the bouncy castle to completely deflate, whilst packing all of the other accessories safely away.

4. Straighten the base and fold the walls neatly inwards including the front step and slide if applicable.

5. Fold one of the long sides to the centre. Walk on the base of the castle to expel air out of vents until flat. Then fold the other long side all the way over to meet far edge. Again walk on base to flatten.

6. Roll slowly and as tightly as possible from the front towards the air vents.

7. Tie around with rope or strap and store safely away.

**Tip: By watching the tutorial youtube video (02) and reading the above, most castles will roll into a fat sausage shape that should fit your chosen vehicle comfortably. However with the bigger units I fold one side in half to the middle, then the other side in half to the middle. I then take one of the halves and fold it again over the other half before I roll otherwise the sausage will be too long for the vehicle.**

HOW TO CARRY OUT MINOR REPAIRS:

If you are in need of repair on bouncy castles the damage may have been caused by too much weight on the castle whilst on hire. Always try to ensure that units aren't being used by anyone over the recommended age. Ensure every customer signs the disclaimer, and that they check the unit over with you when you deliver and with you again when you collect. In the event of any damage being caused during the hire, you will be able to claim back any repair costs directly from the customer as they signed agreeing this condition.

HOW TO CARRY OUT MINOR REPAIRS: (CONT.)

Included with the purchase of each inflatable is usually a repair kit with instructions for use. If not supplied, ask for one as the kit will include patches of the same coloured material used to manufacture the castle, wax-coated string, special glue (HH-66) and curved needles.

The procedure to attach a patch is as follows and if done correctly will hold up quite well.

1. Deflate the unit.

2. Clean the area to be patched, free it from grease, dust etc.

3. Ensure the repair area is flat.

4. Cut the patch (larger than the damaged area) with no sharp edges, (circles work well).

5. Apply the glue to both patch and damaged area. Ensuring you do not spill it on your inflatable.

6. Leave until the glue goes tacky (around 10 minutes).

7. Place a piece of paper on top of the now adhered patch and then a large rag/towel on top of this.

8. Place a heavy weight on top of this and leave for 1 to 2 hours to bond.


USING THREAD TO SEW:


You will need the thread provided for this purpose by the manufacturer, together with a large strong, curved needle. I also use a thimble and pliers or grips.

1. Deflate the unit.

2. Pinch the damaged area together to form a lip.

3. Weave the needle and thread around in a circular fashion over and under USING THE PLIERS OR GRIPS TO FORCE THE NEEDLE THROUGH THE FABRIC of the lip to hold it together.

4. Come backwards with the needle and thread several times to tie off the area and finish.

USING THREAD TO SEW: (CONT.)

For internal or large scale repairs you have several choices. Some upholstery companies who have heavy duty machinery are very competitive for sewing, and you will most likely have one near you. Alternatively you may wish to contact a repair specialist who can collect and redeliver your unit **(Toolbox)**.

RECAP OF SAFETY POINTS:


SET UP

1. Ensure that the fan and cables are positioned safely and that the cables are trailed away and taped down if necessary. Always use a circuit breaker plugged into the mains and test that it is working correctly.

2. Undertake the routine safety check, firstly ensuring the fan plug and cables are intact and that when tested the fan runs correctly. Check that the deflation zips are closed and or deflation tubes are tied off. Do not let the inflation tube become twisted.

3. Nothing is to be placed over the blower restricting the air circulation. Do not let anything block the inlet grill on the fan - windblown paper or plastic litter can be a problem. Position the fan to allow maximum airflow. THE CUSTOMER MUST KEEP CHECKING throughout the period of use, to ensure the fan remains in place and is safely operating.

4. Check that the fan supplies adequate pressure to give a firm footing on the bouncing area and step/front apron.

5. Check the anchor points are secure and intact.

6. Check the seams are intact.

7. Check that all towers and wall to bed seams are intact.

8. Check for any wear and tear. The unit is to be fully intact before any use.

9. The general public/customers are to be kept away until set up is complete.

USAGE

1. The operator of the inflatable (to be a responsible adult) must ensure that the correct age of the child only, is allowed on the unit, and no one over the age specified should be allowed entrance. No more than the recommended number of children to be allowed at any one time. Neither should any height restriction be broken.

2. Socks may be worn but no shoes, spectacles, jewellery or sharp objects.

RECAP OF SAFETY POINTS: (CONT.)

3. The operator is to be positioned at the base of the inflatable where the front step is located;

4. Safety mats should be positioned in front of the inflatable to avoid injury should someone fall off the front step.

5. The operator must be aware that the children should simply bounce up and down, with no climbing, pushing or horseplay. Care must be taken for users to enter at one side and exit at the other. E.g. from the left of the step to enter, and right of the step to exit.

6. Larger more boisterous children should be segregated from the smaller ones.

7. The operator must ensure that the unit remains intact throughout use, in the event of failure of this, all users are to be safely removed. The inflatable must then be restored prior to any continued use. Any accidents must be reported to the Units owner as soon as possible and the injured parties' representative is to sign and date the Accident Log under "the explanation of what occurred".

The unit should not be erected in high winds. The unit must always be secured to the ground with anchor stakes where the ground is suitable. On hard standing some equally effective method, i.e. anchoring to vehicles using strong rope, should be used.

It is essential to only roll and store the inflatable when dry; if the inflatable is stored away wet, the stitching will rot and could damage your inflatable.

HIRING PROCEDURES:

At the back of this manual you will find several forms that we use which you are welcome to copy for your own benefit. We have followed a simple procedure over the years to ensure there are few errors when taking bookings or in completion of deliveries/ collections.

Not only do we hope to make an impression on the phone by being professional and enthusiastic but by using the booking form we aim to collate as much information as possible. Whilst speaking to the customer there should be no doubt in their mind as to the type of castle they have booked and the fee payable on delivery. They should also be made aware of our policy if bad weather occurs and most importantly the times of delivery and collection. As a general guide we aim (but never guarantee) to deliver between the hours of 8am. and noon and start our collections from 4p.m.

HIRING PROCEDURES: (CONT.)

onwards - this tends to suit the majority of our customers but obviously flexibility is the key. Some people may require the inflatable earlier or later than the above. The point is that by stating the "norm" most people who have hired will not ask to keep the castle unreasonably late.

Before ending the phone call the next stage is to notify the customer that we will be posting (or emailing) some paperwork to them. These consist of the hire agreement and our introductory letter which both have identical copies of our terms and conditions on the reverse. The customer is asked to check that all the details are correct and if so to sign and return the hire agreement form only to us in the stamped addressed envelope provided. The use of this process and the cost of two stamps is well worth it.

Following the phone call, the entry is then made in our diary showing the castle booked next to the address of delivery on the date in question. The Order Form is kept in a separate folder and awaits the return of the hire agreement from the customer. Once received they are stapled together and placed in another folder headed "Completions" and the entry in the diary is ticked to confirm the booking.

The system may sound onerous to some but if run efficiently, it allows us to chase any outstanding Hire Agreements and at the same time confirm customers are serious about bookings made! We allow 7 - 10 days for the return of our paperwork and by daily checking the folders we are able to ascertain who is late in responding. We then chase via the phone and if by chance find there has been a change of mind from the customer without informing us, we have the chance to re-hire the unit out again.

More recently I have been emailing the terms and conditions to my customers and then asking them to sign the hire agreement on delivery. This also works well, particularly with late bookings.


DEPOSITS:

I touched on the question of deposits earlier but want to expand on it further. Check what the local competition is doing. If the norm is to take deposits then I advise you to follow suit. The policy I use is that if the castle is cancelled for any reason then the deposit is held by me but the customer is able to use it towards another future booking, provided it happens within 6 months, subject to availability of course. This might be a selling point for you if your competitors do not have a similar strategy!

Credit Cards:

The acceptance of credit cards can make running the business far more efficient. Customers like the fact that they can settle the deposit or the payment straight away via the phone.

Use the yellow pages or google to compare different Credit Card Merchant Services but make sure you compare the fees as they can vary significantly and eat into your profits.

PAPERWORK ON DELIVERY:

THIS SHOULD BE READ IN CONJUNCTION WITH THE TUTORIAL YOUTUBE VIDEO (01) – TOOLBOX.

Once you have arrived at your destination and introduced yourself its time to get to work. Confirm with the customer exactly where they wish the inflatable to be erected and that the point of entry to the castle is agreeable. **Never stake the castle down until the customer is entirely satisfied with its position. I will say that again. Never stake the castle down until the customer is entirely satisfied with its position, particularly the lady of the house. This will save you a lot of time and frustration! Hope I have made my point.** If setting up indoors in a hall for example make sure that no emergency exits are blocked by your equipment.

The form headed "General Rules" is then given to the customer to keep and its contents fully explained. Make certain that there is no doubt as to the potential danger if these simple rules are not followed and enforced. Adult supervision of the castle at all times is the key. Once you are satisfied there is no confusion use the returned 'Hire Agreement' signed by the customer to confirm the time of collection (or if emailed originally ask the customer to sign the 'Hire Agreement' now).

You should now have the "Terms and Conditions" form left. Go through it with the customer and reiterate the main points. Once satisfied ask the customer to carefully read the final section before signing.

You should therefore finish by having two signed forms and the customer should have the "General Rules and Regulations" form. Remember that whether you originally posted or emailed, the customer will also have a copy of your terms and conditions for their records.

As stated earlier, payment is always requested on delivery by but you may decide to choose a different strategy. Finally leave a business card or cards with your contact number on should there be any problems and notify them that your number is also printed on the castle, (which it should be).


SUMMARY:

That's a lot of information to digest so you may want to read it again or listen to the audio. Either way you can always use it as a point of reference for the future.

Most other businesses require premises, expensive equipment, huge insurance fees, staff and all the usual nightmare of business. Not so with this little gem. Start off small and build when ready is my advice and above all have FUN with making as much money as you wish to!

I have included all the forms I personally use in this manual as well as in the **Toolbox** so that you can look at them whilst listening to the **TUTORIAL**  and later add your own details where necessary for printing off.


**I** have tried to cover everything I can think of to help you with your new business venture but I am not infallible. So as promised I am leaving you with my email support address that is available for up to 6 months from the date of purchase of this system. This is designed to get you up and running and I will personally endeavour to answer any questions you may have. Please do not share this information with anyone else as doing so could void this agreement

.

bouncetosuccess@hotmail.com


Finally thank you for your time and the best of luck in starting what I consider to be one of the best little businesses on the planet. I would be very grateful for any constructive feedback you can offer to compliment this manual or any suggested improvements. Testimonials from satisfied customers do make a difference, I assure you.


Best Regards


# Graeme Renwall

# APPENDIX

# ORDER FORM

AGE OF CHILDREN & HOW MANY.......................................................

TYPE OF BOUNCY CASTLE...................................................................

PRICE QUOTED ...................................................................................

DATE OF FUNCTION ............................................................................

TYPE OF FUNCTION & TIME ................................................................

NAME
.............................................................................................................

ADDRESS
.............................................................................................................

.............................................................................................................

.............................................................................................................

EMAIL ADDRESS.................................................................

TELEPHONE NUMBER ........................................................................

MOBILE PHONE NUMBER.................................................................

FUNCTION ADDRESS IF DIFFERENT ................................................

.............................................................................................................

ANY SPECIFIC DIRECTIONS ............................................................

.............................................................................................................

ACCESS, GARDEN SIZE, GRASS, (is it level etc ?) ............................

.............................................................................................................

PREFERRED DELIVERY TIME ............................................................

PREFERRED COLLECTION TIME .......................................................

DATE HIRE AGREEMENT/EMAIL SENT................................................

# (Front of Appendix 1)

(insert header/logo/company name)

Dear

Thank you for your recent enquiry regarding the hire of a (insert name of your company) inflatable. I confirm that (insert type/name of inflatable) and the items listed on the enclosed Hire Agreement have been reserved for you on the (insert date of hire) for the Hire Charge of (insert amount for days hire).

I would be grateful if you could please check the details shown, including the times for delivery and return of the castle, and kindly complete and return the Hire Agreement in the enclosed stamped addressed envelope.

Your reservation can only be held for a maximum of ................ days pending receipt of the signed agreement. A copy of our Terms and Conditions set out on the reverse of the Hire Agreement are also printed on the reverse of this letter for your information and retention. On delivery of the castle we will guide you through our instructions for usage and ask you to sign in confirmation of your agreement.

Should you have any queries at all please do not hesitate to telephone me as I would be pleased to answer any questions you may have.

Thank you for choosing (insert name of your company), we hope you have a great time.

Yours sincerely

*(Back of Appendix 1)*

## **Terms and Conditions**

**Full payment is due at the commencement of the hire period.**

The equipment must be returned in similar condition to that received. Any damage to equipment caused by misuse or neglect or the loss due to removal by non authorised persons shall deem the Hirer liable for full repair or replacement cost plus loss of business. A cleaning charge may be levied if the equipment is excessively soiled.

The equipment must be returned or made available for collection at the time and date agreed, failure to do so will result in additional charges being levied for each extra hire period.

No shoes, jewellery, spectacles, sharp objects or anything else which could injure others or damage the unit is to be worn on the inflatable(s). No food or drink to be taken onto or near the equipment.

Ensure that the equipment is supervised at all times by a responsible adult and that any boisterous behaviour is stopped. Do not allow anyone to sit on the sides, climb, swing or hang from the walls and beams of the inflatable(s). It is strongly recommended that the equipment be under adult supervision whilst in use and that the equipment only to be used for the purpose intended. Do not exceed manufacturer's recommended maximum age of person to use the equipment and never exceed the maximum number also recommended by the manufacturer.

### **No adults should use the inflatable(s) at all.**

All persons using the equipment do so at their own risk.

"(Company Name)' cannot be held responsible for any accidents or injuries to any persons or property arising from the use of the equipment. It is the hirer's responsibility to arrange for adequate insurance where appropriate.
The equipment is to be erected and anchored in accordance with manufacturers instructions by authorised persons of (Company Name) only and should not be used in high winds, storms or extremely wet conditions. This site should be clear of any hazards e.g. glass and stones etc.
"(Company Name)" will endeavour to provide inflatable(s) in a dry condition however on occasions this may be impossible e.g. due to bad weather the day before.

No person shall interfere with the electrical equipment other then the Hirer. The fan should never be turned off when there are any persons using or standing close to the inflatable.

# (Front of Appendix 2)

HIRE AGREEMENT

Name of Hirer ........................................

Date of Hire ............................................
Address .......................................

Address of Venue (if different) ...............................................
...........................................................................................

Email address.................................................................

Tel No's ....................................... .......................................

Hire Charge  (Includes Tax %____) = ........................................

Time required by .....................Time of return ...................................
(We will try and meet your time requirements to the best of our ability)

Equipment Supplied :
Inflatable ....................................................................................
Anchoring Pins No supplied
...................................................................................
Electric Blower ................................................................................
Ground Sheet No supplied
...................................................................................
Residual Current Circuit Breaker (RCD) ....................................................
Extension Cable .................................................................................
Other Equipment.................................................................

Declaration : (Please DO NOT detach - return the complete form - Thank you)
I acknowledge receipt and acceptance of the Terms and Conditions of this Hire
Agreement, the details as listed above and printed overleaf. On delivery of the
castle we will guide you through our instructions for usage and ask you to sign
in confirmation of your agreement.

Signed ............................ Dated ............................................
Name
.......................................................................................................
On behalf of
.......................................................................................................
(School, Church, Organisation, etc.)
Please make cheques payable to ...................................................

*(Back of Appendix 2)*

# Terms and Conditions

**Full payment is due at the commencement of the hire period.**

The equipment must be returned in similar condition to that received. Any damage to equipment caused by misuse or neglect or the loss due to removal by non authorised persons shall deem the Hirer liable for full repair or replacement cost plus loss of business. A cleaning charge may be levied if the equipment is excessively soiled.

The equipment must be returned or made available for collection at the time and date agreed, failure to do so will result in additional charges being levied for each extra hire period.

No shoes, jewellery, spectacles, sharp objects or anything else which could injure others or damage the unit is to be worn on the inflatable(s). No food or drink to be taken onto or near the equipment.

Ensure that the equipment is supervised at all times by a responsible adult and that any boisterous behaviour is stopped. Do not allow anyone to sit on the sides, climb, swing or hang from the walls and beams of the inflatable(s). It is strongly recommended that the equipment be under adult supervision whilst in use and that the equipment only to be used for the purpose intended. Do not exceed manufacturer's recommended maximum age of person to use the equipment and never exceed the maximum number also recommended by the manufacturer.

**No adults should use the inflatable(s) at all.**

All persons using the equipment do so at their own risk.

"(Company Name)' cannot be held responsible for any accidents or injuries to any persons or property arising from the use of the equipment. It is the hirer's responsibility to arrange for adequate insurance where appropriate.
The equipment is to be erected and anchored in accordance with manufacturers instructions by authorised persons of (Company Name) only and should not be used in high winds, storms or extremely wet conditions. This site should be clear of any hazards e.g. glass and stones etc.
"(Company Name)" will endeavour to provide inflatable(s) in a dry condition however on occasions this may be impossible e.g. due to bad weather the day before.

No person shall interfere with the electrical equipment other then the Hirer. The fan should never be turned off when there are any persons using or standing close to the inflatable.

# (Front of Appendix 3)

Item(s)...........................................................................................................
.............................................................................................

Principle Hirer....................................................................................

Address............................................................................................
.................................................................................

The indemnity granted to the supplier under their Public Liability policy will not apply in connection with the legal liability for claims arising out of injury to persons or damage to property, where these terms and conditions are not observed.

**Height:** Nobody who is taller than the outside walls when standing on the bed of the inflatable is allowed to use the equipment.

**Maximum Numbers:** See the maximum numbers recommended for bouncing at any one time listed on the general rules sheet. Please note that the recommendations are a **guideline only** and the final numbers are to be determined by the responsible adult supervising the units.

**Age:** Nobody over the age of ....... is allowed to use the equipment. The supplier should determine the minimum number of attendants needed to operate the device safely and ensure that at least this number is on duty when the device is in operation. The minimum number of adult attendants needed to operate the device safely should be **1.**

**Alcohol and Drugs:** It is required that the supervisor allow that no person under the influence of alcohol or any drugs be allowed to use the equipment at any time.

**Suppliers Responsibility:** If you have any reason to believe that the equipment has not been supplied in accordance with Health & Safety standards, do not sign these Terms and Conditions until you are satisfied the equipment is safe to use.

**Weather:** The above equipment has been designed for use in indoor and outdoor conditions. However when it gets wet, the equipment may become slippery and therefore increase the possibility of injury to the users. In such cases the equipment should not be used. When there are high winds/bad weather then equipment should be deflated.

**Responsibility for Loss or Damage:** The principle hirer accepts full and complete responsibility for all loss or damage to the above stated equipment whilst it is under their custody and control.

# *(Back of Appendix 3)*

## Supplier/erectors responsibilities:-

a) All anchor points are intact and not damaged.
b) Anchor ropes are not worn or chaffed.
c) Anchor stakes and their location remain sound for continued use.
d) The wall to tower fixings are not torn.
e) There are no holes or rips in the surface or seams of the bed and step/front apron/slide.
f) When fully inflated, all walls and towers (when fitted) are firm and upright and the pressure in the bed and step/front apron/slide are sufficient to give a reliable and firm footing.
g) The blower has no exposed wires or loose bolts, screws etc and that the mesh guards over the air inlet and outlet are secured and intact.
h) Electric cables are not worn or chaffed and that plugs, sockets and switches are not damaged.

## Hires/Supervisors responsibilities:-

a) Ensure that all users remove their footwear (socks are OK) and any other hard, sharp or dangerous objects from their persons such as buckles, pens, purses etc.
b) Spectacles are best removed.
c) Not allow anyone to bounce on steps/front apron/slide.
d) Not allow anyone to climb or hang on the outside walls. Not allow users who are taller than the outside walls when standing on the inflated bouncing surface to use the device. The operators should be proactive and take action at the first sign of misbehaviour.
e) Ensure that the equipment is not overloaded, (See General Rules Sheet).
f) Larger or more boisterous children should be segregated from small ones and a number of users at any one time should be limited to that figure which allows each user enough room to play safely.

THE GENERAL RULES HAVE BEEN RECEIVED AND EXPLAINED OUTLINING MAXIMUM RECOMMENDED NUMBERS PER UNIT AND THE RULES REGARDING SLIDE USAGE HAVE ALSO BEEN DISCUSSED AND EXPLAINED.

ANY ACCIDENT OR INJURY HOWEVER MINOR SHOULD BE REPORTED TO THE (COMPANY NAME) REPRESENTATIVE AS SOON AS POSSIBLE WHEREBY THE DETAILS WILL BE DISCUSSED AND ENTERED INTO THE ACCIDENT BOOK LOCATED ON THE VAN.

The undersigned person who confirms that they are over the age of 18, agrees as principle hirer of the above equipment, to enforce the terms and conditions stated on both sides of this paper.

**These terms and conditions to prevail over all others implied or written, at all times.**

Signed.........................................Name.........................................Date.............

*(Front of Appendix 4)*

# **General Rules and Regulations**

- Ensure there are no sharp objects on the ground or adjacent to the area of use.

- No footwear, jewellery, spectacles etc to be worn on the castle.

- No smoking, drinking, eating, sand, face paint, party poppers on or around the castle.

- A responsible adult should supervise the children whilst playing on the castle.

- Do not allow climbing on the walls or any boisterous behaviour.

- Do not mix children of different age groups.

- A circuit breaker should always be used where possible.

- Do not use the castle during heavy, persistent rain or strong winds/bad weather.

- Leave the fan running all the time the castle is in use.

- Check regularly the security of the anchoring pins.

- Please be aware that bouncing in hot weather over a period of time may cause heat exhaustion so it is recommended that fluids are available at all times and that children take breaks to avoid dehydration.

- **Under no circumstances should the Inflatable be moved after the (Your Company Name) representative has left the venue.**

*PLEASE SEE THE GENERAL RULES FOR SLIDE OVERLEAF AND THE MANUFACTURER'S RECOMMENDED NUMBERS OF CHILDREN FOR EACH OF OUR INFLATABLES.*

*(Back of Appendix 4)*

# __GENERAL RULES FOR SLIDE__ *(Back)*

- ONLY 1 USER AT A TIME MAY BE ALLOWED ONTO THE SLIDE IN A CENTRAL POSITION AT THE TOP.
- A FEET-FIRST, SITTING UP OR LYING DOWN POSITION (ON BACKS ONLY) WITH ELBOWS TUCKED IN SHOULD BE INSISTED ON.
- WAVING OF ARMS AND LEGS IS POTENTIALLY UNSAFE.
- TO PREVENT FRICTION BURNS ON EXPOSED SKIN, USERS SHOULD BE FULLY CLOTHED.
- THE BOTTOM OF THE SLIDE MUST BE KEPT UNOBSTRUCTED.
- EACH USER SHOULD MOVE QUICKLY AWAY FROM THE BOTTOM OF THE SLIDE ON ARRIVAL BEFORE THE NEXT USER SLIDES DOWN.
- THE SURFACE OF THE SLIDE MUST BE KEPT CLEAN AND SMOOTH TO ALLOW USERS TO SLIDE FREELY.
- NB.... THERE MUST BE ABSOLUTELY NO JUMPING OR DIVING FROM THE TOP OF THE SLIDE AS THIS COUOLD BE EXTREMELY DANGEROUS TO THE CHILD AND COULD ALSO DAMAGE THE INFLATABLE.

Maximum recommended numbers below are to be used as a guideline only. The supervisor should always start with a smaller number than printed and gauge how busy or empty the unit appears. Maximum and minimums will depend on the age, size and weight of the children so common sense is required.

**EXAMPLE:  JUMPING CASTLE (3m X 3.66m)**
RECOMMENDED MAXIMUM AGE 6......6 CHILDREN AT ANY ONE TIME.

**EXAMPLE:  BOX SLIDE JUMPING CASTLE (3.66m X 5.18m)**
RECOMMENDED MAXIMUM AGE 10.......6 CHILDREN AT ANY ONE TIME.

**EXAMPLE: JUNGLE JUMPING CASTLE (3.66m X 4.27m)**
RECOMMENDED MAXIMUM AGE 11.......8 CHILDREN AT ANY ONE TIME.

**EXAMPLE: ARCH WITH SLIDE COMBO (5.18m X 4.27m)**
RECOMMENDED MAXIMUM AGE 10......8 CHILDREN AT ANY ONE TIME.

**EXAMPLE: CLASS BOUNCER (4.57m X 4.88m)**
RECOMMENDED MAXIMUM AGE 14......10 CHILDREN AT ANY ONE TIME.

**Itinerary Date:**_____

| Delivery Time | Castle | Name & Address | Map Ref: | Money to be collected. | Pickup Time |
|---|---|---|---|---|---|
|  |  |  |  |  |  |
|  |  |  |  |  |  |
|  |  |  |  |  |  |
|  |  |  |  |  |  |
|  |  |  |  |  |  |
|  |  |  |  |  |  |
|  |  |  |  |  |  |
|  |  |  |  |  |  |
|  |  |  |  |  |  |

# Welcome To The TOOLBOX

I have included as many useful tools as I can think of to help you start your new business. My mission is to save you time and money so have a browse and let me know what you think at bouncetosuccess@hotmail.com

Thank you once again and the Best of Luck!

The first place I want to share with you provides the following on a regular basis:-

## These items are sure to jumpstart your business!

| | | | |
|---|---|---|---|
| Premium Business Cards | **Now FREE** | Two Tone Cotton Bag | **Now 65% OFF** |
| Postcards | **Now FREE** | FREE Banner | **Great Value** |
| Brochures | **Now FREE** | Flyers | **Now FREE** |
| T-Shirt | **Now FREE** | Return Address Labels | **Now FREE** |
| Free Lawn Sign | **Great Value** | Rack Cards | **Now FREE** |
| Letterhead with matching envelope | **Now FREE** | Free Rubber Stamp | **Great Value** |
| Free Sticky Notes | **Great Value** | Website | **One month FREE trial** |
| Free Pen | **Great Value** | Presentation Folders | **Now 33% OFF** |
| Magnets | **Now FREE** | Announcements | **Now FREE** |
| Free Mouse Mat | **Great Value** | Note Pad | **Now FREE** |
| Note Cards | **Now FREE** | Free Cotton Bag | **Great Value** |
| Invitations | **Now FREE** | Stamp Ink Pad | **Now 25% OFF** |
| Free Key ring | **Great Value** | Large Stamp | **Now Half Price** |
| Uploads | **Now Half Price** | XL Photo Magnet | **Now FREE** |
| Thank You Cards | **Now FREE** | Business Card Holder | **Now Half Price** |
| 2009 Calendar Magnets | **Now FREE** | Free Logo Design | **Great Value** |
| Poster | **Now FREE** | 2009 Photo Wall Calendar | **Now FREE** |
| Small Window Decal | **Now FREE** | Wallet Calendars | **Now Half Price** |
| Long Sleeved T-Shirt | **Now Half Price** | Signature Stamp | **Now Half Price** |
| Large Car Door Magnet | **Now 75% OFF** | 2009 Desk Calendar | **Now FREE** |

This company sends emails like this to me every day. You can join for free. You can choose and design your own logo for free.
You can wear your own T-Shirt with your logo for free, (perfect for marketing).
You can get your own business cards for free.
You can get your own postcards and brochures for free.
You can get your "Happy Birthday Fridge Magnets" for free.
How about a free "Lawn Sign" near the castle?
Letterhead with matching envelope for free.
Flyers for free.
Large Car Door Magnets at 75% off.

The list is endless. They also send other offers which include a baseball cap with your logo for free. You do have to pay for postage for each item, (they have to make some money), but it has to be one of the cheapest options I have ever seen to help jumpstart your business.

Please also note that they do provide a website service, in this case with a free trial period. This is the cheaper option I mentioned in the manual. Why not give it a try and see what you think? **It's FREE**.

Simply copy and paste the following into your browser and it will lead you to this little goldmine starting with free business cards. Remember to click on the "select a country" tab located at the top of the web page:

**http://tiny.cc/qIrFU**

**THE WEB:**

The next item relates to those of you who would prefer to build their own website(s). They **Guarantee** that this is the easiest way to create Professional Quality Web Sites and I must agree. But don't take my word for it, copy this into your browser **http://tiny.cc/6uMhp** and click on 'watch the video' to make up your own mind.........

Other links of use:
www.hostgator.com
www.needanarticle.com
www.adwords.google.com
www.elance.com
Most Blogs or Ezines are usually free and **will** bring traffic to your website. There are a mass of online advertising companies that are also free so Google your area and get your company name or advert registered.

I mentioned in my manual one of the best forms of advertising on the planet. The answer is eBay which ranks highly with the search engines and has brought me a lot of business. In some countries you are able to place a classified advert for free with eBay but even if you pay for an advert once a month, the cost is minimal but in my opinion well worth it.

Other well ranked sites are: Twitter and Squidoo.

## Procedure For Taking An Order:

Follow the order form completing as much information as possible. Two phone numbers, including mobile where possible, are a must.

I always ask the following at the start of the conversation:

How can I help you?
May I ask whereabouts you live or where the venue is?
What date were you looking to book for? (Assumptive Close).
How did you find me? (Market Research).
What ages are the children likely to be, maximum and minimum?
What are the times of the party?
Have you already found what you are looking for on the web site or would you like some advice?
They will probably ask the cost at this point so be competitive and confident that the deal is second to none.

**The longer the customer is on the phone and the more questions you ask (within reason), the better! Be yourself and have a natter but don't bore them to death.**

Once the customer has made a choice, check availability and if the inflatable is free for hire, tell them "that it's theirs if they want it".
If they proceed then complete the rest of the Order Form and explain how you work. How and why you take deposits. It's to deter time wasters but if cancelled due to the weather or illness then you may use the deposit towards a future event and the price remains the same, subject to availability. If the fault is yours due to the vehicle breaking down for example then the deposit is refunded but this is extremely rare.

Explain that you provide the extension leads but you will need a plug socket. (Some people may think you carry your own generator).
Find out how far from the house they are thinking of positioning the unit as this could cost you time.

Always give yourself a range of times for delivery, e.g. 7 to 10 a.m. but nearer the date you will text, email or call them to give a more accurate time. **Always give a range of at least one hour though.**

Collection should be guided by you. Suggest an hour after the party finishes but use the words onwards, e.g. 4p.m. onwards.
Check that the customer has adequate space for the unit.
If they wish to check with their partner first for example then tell them you can hold it for 24 hours if they wish but please could they let you know either way.

--------------------------------------------------------------------------------

**NEVER DOUBLE BOOK A CASTLE.**
**I have heard that some people do this but if you are taking deposits there is no need. Even if you decide not to take a deposit, this practice is totally unprofessional particularly when you consider you are letting down children.**

So now you have your bookings for the weekend. Around Wednesday or Thursday I start to map out the itinerary and complete the paperwork. In order, I will have the Google map with directions at the top, followed by the order form. Next will be Appendix 2, then Appendix 3 and finally at the back will be The General Rules, (Appendix 4). All these should be stapled together so that on arrival you can pull off the General Rules for the customer to keep after the inflatable has been set up and checked. Once the rules have been explained the customer should sign Appendix 2 and Appendix 3 which **YOU** keep. They should already have a copy or an email of your terms and conditions.

**Hopefully you have your mobile telephone number printed on the inflatable but if not, make sure the customer has a number they can contact you on in case of emergency.**

I then complete the **Main Itinerary Form** which helps me to load the vehicle by starting from the bottom of the list. Personally I start by placing the fans in their boxes along the front of the vehicle behind the seats. I then roll the first castle, (the last one to be delivered) on its side up to the fans to hold them securely. The remaining castles are placed upright against the first castle. This maximises the space available and allows you to place the safety mats on top of the first castle and the fans. I keep all the extension leads, circuit breakers, stakes, mallet and other bits and pieces in a large plastic box which along with the trolley are the last items to be loaded.

------------------------------------------------------------------------

**Ensure that the trolley or sack barrow is loaded in such a way that should you need to stop suddenly, it will not go flying out the back.**

------------------------------------------------

### WARNING

**Remember to keep all the relevant details of the booking, e.g. name, address, type of castle and contact phone numbers in the Main Diary in case you lose the order forms AND use a specific place or wallet where you can carefully store the monies due on collection as most will pay with cash.**

### THE JUGGLING ACT

Useful if you are renting out a lot of castles. Most people will take delivery the day before, something for nothing. Some may be concerned by the weather so again state that if they are unable to use the castle then they will not be charged. On collection you have the option to leave the castle until the following day but check the weather forecast in case rain is due. If this is the case then I would rather work late and get them in dry.

## WHEN TO ADD MORE INFLATABLES

This will depend on your budget of course but putting some of your profits aside for expansion makes good sense, particularly if you are inundated with calls. Be aware of what your market is asking for as this will help you to decide what to buy in the future. Allow at least 2-3 months when placing an order before your prime rental season begins where possible.

## JOINING ORGANISATIONS

When you get bigger perhaps or want to break into the corporate market, joining organisations such as the IAAPA (www.iaapa.org) can certainly help your profile and keep you abreast of the latest news and views. The other great advantage is that if you are allowed to link to their website, this will improve your page ranking and thus increase the traffic to your web site. Check the annual fee and if you feel it's too expensive now, wait until you become more established.

## WHAT YOU NEED TO START
- A Federal Tax ID number, V.A.T. number, G.S.T. number or the appropriate government tax reference pertaining to your country. This will allow you to buy from vendors at wholesale rates.
- A phone number dedicated to the business with divert facility and an answering machine.
- A website showing the relevant pictures and prices of your goods for hire giving 24 hour access to any potential customers. This should include your contact numbers and email address for any enquiries.
- Computer.

- Printer.
- Paper.
- Envelopes.
- Pens and lots of them!
- Filing cabinet specifically for the business.
- Calculator.
- Stapler and Paper Clips.
- Sticky tape.
- Master Diary
- A plastic folder to keep your paperwork in transit with at least two pens, blank photocopies of all the appendices and marketing materials such as business cards and fridge magnets.
- Heavy duty extension leads of varying lengths up to 50 feet (15m approx).
- Mallet x 2 (good to carry spare).
- Sandbags and/or weights to secure castle where there is no grass to stake the inflatable down, (see eBay).
- Several metres of strong tie rope
- Electrical adapters.
- Circuit Breakers.
- Repair Kit: curved needles, special glue (HH-66) & wax-coated string/thread
- Screwdriver set and spare fuses.
- Groundsheets/Tarpaulins.
- Cleaning Products (see later).
- Trolley or sack barrow, (keeping a spare at home is very useful).
- Rolls of different coloured Duct Tape.
- Large Battery Operated Torch.
- Good quality Map of the local area.

## That should do you for now!
## QUESTIONS TO ASK THE MANUFACTURER BEFORE BUYING

Is the unit suitable for commercial rental purposes?
Is it made from Commercial Grade PVC Coated Fire-Retardant Vinyl?
Is it Double-Stitched throughout inside and out?
Is it sewn with a thick coated NYLON string that withstands deterioration over time and weather?

You ask the above because:
- Your **State** or **Country** may require it by law.
- Your **Insurer** may require it before covering you.
- The heavier the material the better for durability.
- You want to see whether your manufacturer is concerned with reasonable quality and of course safety measures.

What does the TOTAL QUOTED PRICE include?

- Does it include the AIR BLOWER(S) OR ELECTRIC FAN(S)?
- Does it include all delivery costs e.g. Shipping and Handling?
- Does it include Stakes, Groundsheets or Tarps, Anchor Points, Tie-Down Ropes, Repair Kits and Item-Specific Safety Instructions e.g. Maximum Age Limits and Recommended Maximum Numbers to use?
- How long is the WARRANTY and what exactly does it cover?
- Are there any other hidden costs e.g. for specific safety code regulations?
- What discounts are currently available?
- Do they have a list of INSURANCE PROVIDERS AND FINANCE/LEASE COMPANY sources for their equipment. This may save you a lot of time searching but it's also a good test as to whether the company is "on the ball".

**PLEASE DO ASK THESE QUESTIONS AS COMPANIES WANT TO SELL YOU THEIR STOCK AND SHOULD BE ONLY TOO PLEASED TO PROVIDE THIS INFORMATION.**

## CLEANING PRODUCTS

The following should also be stored on your vehicle for cleaning purposes:-

- Powerful portable electric vacuum to clean out leaves and dirt.
- Simple Green cleaning solution (or similar product) diluted with water, 1 cup of Simple Green per 2 gal. of water.
- Sponges, cloths and towels.
- Son Of A Gun or Armor All Protectant for a light shine on the outside of the unit, (or similar product).
- Lysol disinfectant (or similar product) diluted in a spray bottle for a fresh smell inside the unit. Occasionally you may find that the inflatables attract a nasty odour e.g. if left rolled up wet for a long period of time. Spray a good amount of Lysol (or similar) directly

into the intake of the blower motor while it is running so that it gets INSIDE the unit to disinfect the smell.

**Try and clean each unit after each rental as you don't want to turn up to the next venue with a dirty or smelly castle. This will not give the customer the best impression and could lose you future business.**

## BOLT ON RENTAL EQUIPMENT

### Concession Supplies

- Gold Medal Products Co. – www.gmpopcorn.com                     (800) 543-0862
- Great Western Products Company – www.gwproducts.com       (800) 2392143
- Sam's Club – www.samsclub.com
  (888) 7467726

### Cotton Candy Supplies

- Gold Medal Products Co. – As above
- Great Western Products Company – As above

### Popcorn Supplies

- Gold Medal Products Co. – As above
- Great Western Products Company – As above
- Sysco (800) 7863001
- Sam's Club – See Above

## Shaved Ice & Snow-Cone Machines

- Gold Medal Products Co. – As above
- Great Western Products Company – As above
- National Fruit Flavor Company Inc. – www.nationalfruitflavor.com (800) 9661123
- Ralph's SnoBall Supply inc. – www.snowballssupply.com (877) 5437997
- Sam's Club – As above

## Tables and Chairs
- Sam's Club – See Above

**May I suggest that before buying anything, you take a look at eBay first.**

## CHECKING THE NAME OF YOUR BUSINESS

For the federal trademark search go to www.uspto.gov/

## Insurance Requirements

Inflatables are extremely safe but accidents can happen occasionally. You are responsible for ensuring that the equipment is safe to use but it's always advisable to insure yourself against potential claims. **In some countries Public Liability Insurance is legally required.**

Here are some insurance companies, in no particular order, who deal with the rental industry but if you call them and they no longer offer this service, ask them if they know who does.

- St. Pauls Ins.      (800) 2419245
- Interwest          (916) 6098422
- Friedman Group   (877) 5807066
- Dsanctis Ins.      (781) 935 8480
- Dick Wardlow Ins. (800) 2983000
- Cornerstone               (714)  4900500
- Cole Humphrey    (419) 6348010
- Byrne Risk Mgmt. (949) 2303195
- Altemeier-Oliver   (513) 9845335

- Acordia                     (952)  8303039
- Evolution Ins.          (800)  3211493
- Int.Special Events (800)  3211493
- Haas & Wilkerson (800)  8217703
- K & K Insurance    (800)  6486406
- Scottsdale            (800)  4237675
- Ardi                      (800)  8216580
- Cossio Ins. Agency      (864)  8622838
- Mulvey Insurance (866)  8567070
- Cole Humphrey     (419)  634 8010
- Int. Speciality Ins.(800)  521 1709
- Isner                    (614)  2368691
- JBL Trinity           (405)  2168118
- JT Lake                (916)  3383277
- Neil Oliver           (770)  4786548
- NSERA                (864)  2979727
- Showmen             (847)  6761444
- Speciality Ins.      (864)  2979727
- Sterling & Sterling     (516)  7738673
- Waterfield            (800)  2846687

## Manufacturers of Inflatables

If you are on a tight budget, some of the following companies may offer used equipment for sale as a cheaper alternative. Although I prefer buying brand new, this may suit some of you as a kind of test-drive option.

www.cuttingedgecreations.com
www.clowningaround.net
www.moonwalks4sale.com
www.theinflatablestore.com
www.eventgames.com
www.misterinflatable.com
www.ninjajump.com
www.adventure-bounce.com
www.biginflatablethings.com
www.einflatables.com
www.funequipment.com
www.happyjump.com
www.inlatabledepot.com
www.inflatable2000.com
www.jumpingthings.com
www.magicjump.com
www.moon-walker.com
www.bigairjumphouses.com

## Importing Options

**I have used the following two companies which are based in the U.K. and would strongly recommend them as I know that both provide quality inflatables that will last for a long time. Bee Tee is not the cheapest manufacturer but the speed of their delivery and the range on offer is second to none. Designer Bounce is extremely competitive and although delivery may take longer, the owner is a man of his word which unfortunately seems to be rare these days. You will have to weigh up the pros and cons of importing but a lot of the expenses incurred can probably be reclaimed. Again I urge you to seek advice on all tax affairs in your state or country.**

**www.beetee.co.uk**

**www.designerbounce.co.uk**

# ORDER FORM

AGE OF CHILDREN & HOW MANY.................................................................

TYPE OF BOUNCY CASTLE.......................................................................

PRICE QUOTED .....................................................................................

DATE OF FUNCTION ..............................................................................

TYPE OF FUNCTION & TIME ....................................................................

NAME ...................................................................................................

ADDRESS ..............................................................................................

.............................................................................................................

.............................................................................................................

EMAIL ADDRESS.....................................................................

TELEPHONE NUMBER .............................................................................

MOBILE PHONE NUMBER..........................................................

FUNCTION ADDRESS IF DIFFERENT ........................................................

.............................................................................................................

ANY SPECIFIC DIRECTIONS ....................................................................

.............................................................................................................

ACCESS, GARDEN SIZE, GRASS, (is it level etc ?) .....................................

.............................................................................................................

PREFERRED DELIVERY TIME ...................................................................

PREFERRED COLLECTION TIME ..............................................................

DATE HIRE AGREEMENT/EMAIL SENT.....................................................

# (Front of Appendix 1)

(insert header/logo/company name)


Dear

Thank you for your recent enquiry regarding the hire of a (insert name of your company) inflatable. I confirm that (insert type/name of inflatable) and the items listed on the enclosed Hire Agreement have been reserved for you on the (insert date of hire) for the Hire Charge of (insert amount for days hire).

I would be grateful if you could please check the details shown, including the times for delivery and return of the castle, and kindly complete and return the Hire Agreement in the enclosed stamped addressed envelope.

Your reservation can only be held for a maximum of ................ days pending receipt of the signed agreement. A copy of our Terms and Conditions set out on the reverse of the Hire Agreement are also printed on the reverse of this letter for your information and retention. On delivery of the castle we will guide you through our instructions for usage and ask you to sign in confirmation of your agreement.

Should you have any queries at all please do not hesitate to telephone me as I would be pleased to answer any questions you may have.

Thank you for choosing (insert name of your company), we hope you have a great time.

Yours sincerely

*(Back of Appendix 1)*

# Terms and Conditions

**Full payment is due at the commencement of the hire period.**

The equipment must be returned in similar condition to that received. Any damage to equipment caused by misuse or neglect or the loss due to removal by non authorised persons shall deem the Hirer liable for full repair or replacement cost plus loss of business. A cleaning charge may be levied if the equipment is excessively soiled.

The equipment must be returned or made available for collection at the time and date agreed, failure to do so will result in additional charges being levied for each extra hire period.

No shoes, jewellery, spectacles, sharp objects or anything else which could injure others or damage the unit is to be worn on the inflatable(s). No food or drink to be taken onto or near the equipment.

Ensure that the equipment is supervised at all times by a responsible adult and that any boisterous behaviour is stopped. Do not allow anyone to sit on the sides, climb, swing or hang from the walls and beams of the inflatable(s). It is strongly recommended that the equipment be under adult supervision whilst in use and that the equipment only to be used for the purpose intended. Do not exceed manufacturer's recommended maximum age of person to use the equipment and never exceed the maximum number also recommended by the manufacturer.

**No adults should use the inflatable(s) at all.**

All persons using the equipment do so at their own risk.

"(Company Name)' cannot be held responsible for any accidents or injuries to any persons or property arising from the use of the equipment. It is the hirer's responsibility to arrange for adequate insurance where appropriate.
The equipment is to be erected and anchored in accordance with manufacturers instructions by authorised persons of (Company Name) only and should not be used in high winds, storms or extremely wet conditions. This site should be clear of any hazards e.g. glass and stones etc.
"(Company Name)" will endeavour to provide inflatable(s) in a dry condition however on occasions this may be impossible e.g. due to bad weather the day before.

No person shall interfere with the electrical equipment other then the Hirer. The fan should never be turned off when there are any persons using or standing close to the inflatable.

*(Front of Appendix 2)*

HIRE AGREEMENT

Name of Hirer ...................................... Date of Hire ..............................................
Address .........................................

Address of Venue (if different).............................................
.................................................................................................................
.................................................................

Email address................................................................................

Tel No's ......................................... ..............................................

Hire Charge  (Includes Tax %____) = .........................................

Time required by ..................................... Time of return .........................................
(We will try and meet your time requirements to the best of our ability)

Equipment Supplied :
Inflatable
.................................................................................................................
Anchoring Pins No supplied
.................................................................................................
Electric Blower
.................................................................................................................
Ground Sheet No supplied
.................................................................................................
Residual Current Circuit Breaker (RCD) ..................................................................
Extension Cable
.................................................................................................
Other
Equipment.................................................................................................................

Declaration: (Please DO NOT detach - return the complete form - Thank you)
I acknowledge receipt and acceptance of the Terms and Conditions of this Hire
Agreement, the details as listed above and printed overleaf. On delivery of the
castle we will guide you through our instructions for usage and ask you to sign
in confirmation of your agreement.

Signed ...................................................... Dated .................
.................................................................
Name
.................................................................................................................
On behalf of
.................................................................................................................
(School, Church, Organisation, etc.)
Please make cheques payable to ...................................................

*(Back of Appendix 2)*

# **Terms and Conditions**

## **Full payment is due at the commencement of the hire period.**

The equipment must be returned in similar condition to that received. Any damage to equipment caused by misuse or neglect or the loss due to removal by non authorised persons shall deem the Hirer liable for full repair or replacement cost plus loss of business. A cleaning charge may be levied if the equipment is excessively soiled.

The equipment must be returned or made available for collection at the time and date agreed, failure to do so will result in additional charges being levied for each extra hire period.

No shoes, jewellery, spectacles, sharp objects or anything else which could injure others or damage the unit is to be worn on the inflatable(s). No food or drink to be taken onto or near the equipment.

Ensure that the equipment is supervised at all times by a responsible adult and that any boisterous behaviour is stopped. Do not allow anyone to sit on the sides, climb, swing or hang from the walls and beams of the inflatable(s). It is strongly recommended that the equipment be under adult supervision whilst in use and that the equipment only to be used for the purpose intended. Do not exceed manufacturer's recommended maximum age of person to use the equipment and never exceed the maximum number also recommended by the manufacturer.

## **No adults should use the inflatable(s) at all.**

All persons using the equipment do so at their own risk.

"(Company Name)' cannot be held responsible for any accidents or injuries to any persons or property arising from the use of the equipment. It is the hirer's responsibility to arrange for adequate insurance where appropriate.
The equipment is to be erected and anchored in accordance with manufacturers instructions by authorised persons of (Company Name) only and should not be used in high winds, storms or extremely wet conditions. This site should be clear of any hazards e.g. glass and stones etc.
"(Company Name)" will endeavour to provide inflatable(s) in a dry condition however on occasions this may be impossible e.g. due to bad weather the day before.

No person shall interfere with the electrical equipment other then the Hirer. The fan should never be turned off when there are any persons using or standing close to the inflatable.

## *(Front of Appendix 3)*

Item(s)............................................................................................................
...................................................................................................................

Principle Hirer..............................................................................................

Address.........................................................................................................
...................................................................................................................

The indemnity granted to the supplier under their Public Liability policy will not apply in connection with the legal liability for claims arising out of injury to persons or damage to property, where these terms and conditions are not observed.

**Height:** Nobody who is taller than the outside walls when standing on the bed of the inflatable is allowed to use the equipment.

**Maximum Numbers:** See the maximum numbers recommended for bouncing at any one time listed on the general rules sheet. Please note that the recommendations are a **guideline only** and the final numbers are to be determined by the responsible adult supervising the units.

**Age:** Nobody over the age of ....... is allowed to use the equipment. The supplier should determine the minimum number of attendants needed to operate the device safely and ensure that at least this number is on duty when the device is in operation. The minimum number of adult attendants needed to operate the device safely should be **1.**

**Alcohol and Drugs:** It is required that the supervisor allow that no person under the influence of alcohol or any drugs be allowed to use the equipment at any time.

**Suppliers Responsibility:** If you have any reason to believe that the equipment has not been supplied in accordance with Health & Safety standards, do not sign these Terms and Conditions until you are satisfied the equipment is safe to use.

**Weather:** The above equipment has been designed for use in indoor and outdoor conditions. However when it gets wet, the equipment may become slippery and therefore increase the possibility of injury to the users. In such cases the equipment should not be used. When there are high winds/bad weather then equipment should be deflated.

**Responsibility for Loss or Damage:** The principle hirer accepts full and complete responsibility for all loss or damage to the above stated equipment whilst it is under their custody and control.

# *(Back of Appendix 3)*
## Supplier/erectors responsibilities:-

i)   All anchor points are intact and not damaged.
j)   Anchor ropes are not worn or chaffed.
k)   Anchor stakes and their location remain sound for continued use.
l)   The wall to tower fixings are not torn.
m)   There are no holes or rips in the surface or seams of the bed and step/front apron/slide.
n)   When fully inflated, all walls and towers (when fitted) are firm and upright and the pressure in the bed and step/front apron/slide are sufficient to give a reliable and firm footing.
o)   The blower has no exposed wires or loose bolts, screws etc and that the mesh guards over the air inlet and outlet are secured and intact.
p)   Electric cables are not worn or chaffed and that plugs, sockets and switches are not damaged.

## Hires/Supervisors responsibilities:-

g)   Ensure that all users remove their footwear (socks are OK) and any other hard, sharp or dangerous objects from their persons such as buckles, pens, purses etc.
h)   Spectacles are best removed.
i)   Not allow anyone to bounce on steps/front apron/slide.
j)   Not allow anyone to climb or hang on the outside walls. Not allow users who are taller than the outside walls when standing on the inflated bouncing surface to use the device. The operators should be proactive and take action at the first sign of misbehaviour.
k)   Ensure that the equipment is not overloaded  (See General Rules Sheet).
l)   Larger or more boisterous children should be segregated from small ones and a number of users at any one time should be limited to that figure which allows each user enough room to play safely.

THE GENERAL RULES HAVE BEEN RECEIVED AND EXPLAINED OUTLINING MAXIMUM RECOMMENDED NUMBERS PER UNIT AND THE RULES REGARDING SLIDE USAGE HAVE ALSO BEEN DISCUSSED AND EXPLAINED.

ANY ACCIDENT OR INJURY HOWEVER MINOR SHOULD BE REPORTED TO THE (COMPANY NAME) REPRESENTATIVE AS SOON AS POSSIBLE WHEREBY THE DETAILS WILL BE DISCUSSED AND ENTERED INTO THE ACCIDENT BOOK LOCATED ON THE VAN.

The undersigned person who confirms that they are over the age of 18, agrees as principle hirer of the above equipment, to enforce the terms and conditions stated on both sides of this paper.

**These terms and conditions to prevail over all others implied or written, at all times.**

Signed............................................Name............................................Date..............

# **General Rules and Regulations**

- Ensure there are no sharp objects on the ground or adjacent to the area of use.

- No footwear, jewellery, spectacles etc to be worn on the castle.

- No smoking, drinking, eating, sand, face paint, party poppers on or around the castle.

- A responsible adult should supervise the children whilst playing on the castle.

- Do not allow climbing on the walls or any boisterous behaviour.

- Do not mix children of different age groups.

- A circuit breaker should always be used where possible.

- Do not use the castle during heavy, persistent rain or strong winds/bad weather.

- Leave the fan running all the time the castle is in use.

- Check regularly the security of the anchoring pins.

- Please be aware that bouncing in hot weather over a period of time may cause heat exhaustion so it is recommended that fluids are available at all times and that children take breaks to avoid dehydration.

- **Under no circumstances should the Inflatable be moved after the (Your Company Name) representative has left the venue.**

*PLEASE SEE THE GENERAL RULES FOR SLIDE OVERLEAF AND THE MANUFACTURER'S RECOMMENDED NUMBERS OF CHILDREN FOR EACH OF OUR INFLATABLES.*

# **GENERAL RULES FOR SLIDE** *(Back)*

- ONLY 1 USER AT A TIME MAY BE ALLOWED ONTO THE SLIDE IN A CENTRAL POSITION AT THE TOP.
- A FEET-FIRST, SITTING UP OR LYING DOWN POSITION (ON BACKS ONLY) WITH ELBOWS TUCKED IN SHOULD BE INSISTED ON.
- WAVING OF ARMS AND LEGS IS POTENTIALLY UNSAFE.
- TO PREVENT FRICTION BURNS ON EXPOSED SKIN, USERS SHOULD BE FULLY CLOTHED.
- THE BOTTOM OF THE SLIDE MUST BE KEPT UNOBSTRUCTED.
- EACH USER SHOULD MOVE QUICKLY AWAY FROM THE BOTTOM OF THE SLIDE ON ARRIVAL BEFORE THE NEXT USER SLIDES DOWN.
- THE SURFACE OF THE SLIDE MUST BE KEPT CLEAN AND SMOOTH TO ALLOW USERS TO SLIDE FREELY.
- NB.... THERE MUST BE ABSOLUTELY NO JUMPING OR DIVING FROM THE TOP OF THE SLIDE AS THIS COUOLD BE EXTREMELY DANGEROUS TO THE CHILD AND COULD ALSO DAMAGE THE INFLATABLE.

Maximum recommended numbers below are to be used as a guideline only. The supervisor should always start with a smaller number than printed and gauge how busy or empty the unit appears. Maximum and minimums will depend on the age, size and weight of the children so common sense is required.

**EXAMPLE:  JUMPING CASTLE (3m X 3.66m)**
RECOMMENDED MAXIMUM AGE 6......6 CHILDREN AT ANY ONE TIME.

**EXAMPLE:  BOX SLIDE JUMPING CASTLE (3.66m X 5.18m)**
RECOMMENDED MAXIMUM AGE 10.......6 CHILDREN AT ANY ONE TIME.

**EXAMPLE: JUNGLE JUMPING CASTLE (3.66m X 4.27m)**
RECOMMENDED MAXIMUM AGE 11.......8 CHILDREN AT ANY ONE TIME.

**EXAMPLE: ARCH WITH SLIDE COMBO (5.18m X 4.27m)**
RECOMMENDED MAXIMUM AGE 10......8 CHILDREN AT ANY ONE TIME.

**EXAMPLE: CLASS BOUNCER (4.57m X 4.88m)**
RECOMMENDED MAXIMUM AGE 14......10 CHILDREN AT ANY ONE TIME.

**Itinerary Date:**_____

| Delivery Time | Castle | Name & Address | Map Ref: | Money to be collected. | Pickup Time |
|---|---|---|---|---|---|
| | | | | | |
| | | | | | |
| | | | | | |
| | | | | | |
| | | | | | |
| | | | | | |
| | | | | | |
| | | | | | |
| | | | | | |

# Finally

I hope that you have enjoyed this programme.

I've done my absolute best to give you an overview and much of the detail of this exciting business.

Of course I could have gone on and on as the questions you may have are unlimited. But I wanted this manual to be a sensible size, not a telephone directory! And the truth is, once you're fired up about making this happen in YOUR life, you'll find the answers you need to fill in any gaps I may have left.

This really is possible if you take what I have disclosed in this manual and build upon it with your own researches and effort.

Above all, please don't just put this manual to one side and think something like: "That was great. I'm really going to do that... one day."

Don't put this off until tomorrow.

Do it now!

My very best wishes for your future success.

**Graeme Renwall**

**YOUTUBE VIDEO (01)**
**COPY & PASTE THE FOLLOWING LINK INTO YOUR BROWSER**
**http://youtu.be/E5L87Yf-IPo**

**YOUTUBE VIDEO (2)**
**COPY & PASTE THE FOLLOWING LINK INTO YOUR BROWSER**
**http://youtu.be/qtywfLsEDB0**

5411025R10045

Made in the USA
San Bernardino, CA
05 November 2013